Making the MOVE

PROPERTY OF
THE PILGRIM LIBRARY
THE DEFIANCE COLLEGE

DEFIANCE, OHIO

WITHDRAWN
PILGRIM LIBRARY

by the same author

The Red Beast
Controlling Anger in Children with Asperger's Syndrome
K.I. Al-Ghani
Illustrated by Haitham Al-Ghani
ISBN 978 1 84310 943 3

of related interest

How to Make School Make Sense
A Parents' Guide to Helping the Child with Asperger Syndrome
Clare Lawrence
Foreword by Tony Attwood
ISBN 978 1 84310 664 7

Girls Growing Up on the Autism Spectrum
What Parents and Professionals Should Know About the Pre-Teen and Teenage Years
Shana Nichols with Gina Marie Moravcik and Samara Pulver Tetenbaum
ISBN 978 1 84310 855 9

Reaching and Teaching the Child with Autism Spectrum Disorder
Using Learning Preferences and Strengths
Heather MacKenzie
ISBN 978 1 84310 623 4

Hints and Tips for Helping Children with Autism Spectrum Disorders
Useful Strategies for Home, School, and the Community
Dion E. Betts and Nancy J. Patrick
ISBN 978 1 84310 896 2

Create a Reward Plan for Your Child with Asperger Syndrome
John Smith, Jane Donlan and Bob Smith
ISBN 978 1 84310 622 7

PROPERTY OF

THE PILGRIM LIBRARY
THE DEFIANCE COLLEGE
DEFIANCE, OHIO

WITHDRAWN
PILGRIM LIBRARY

Making the MOVE

A Guide for Schools and Parents on
the Transfer of Pupils with Autism
Spectrum Disorders (ASDs) from
Primary to Secondary School

K.I. Al-Ghani and Lynda Kenward
Illustrated by Haitham Al-Ghani

Jessica Kingsley Publishers
London and Philadelphia

First published in 2009
by Jessica Kingsley Publishers
116 Pentonville Road
London N1 9JB, UK
and
400 Market Street, Suite 400
Philadelphia, PA 19106, USA

www.jkp.com

Copyright © K.I. Al-Ghani and Lynda Kenward 2009
Illustrator copyright © Haitham Al-Ghani 2009

All rights reserved. No part of this publication may be reproduced in any material form (including photocopying or storing it in any medium by electronic means and whether or not transiently or incidentally to some other use of this publication) without the written permission of the copyright owner except in accordance with the provisions of the Copyright, Designs and Patents Act 1988 or under the terms of a licence issued by the Copyright Licensing Agency Ltd, Saffron House, 6–10 Kirby Street, London EC1N 8TS. Applications for the copyright owner's written permission to reproduce any part of this publication should be addressed to the publisher.

Warning: The doing of an unauthorised act in relation to a copyright work may result in both a civil claim for damages and criminal prosecution.

All pages marked ✓ may be photocopied for personal use, but may not be reproduced for any other purposes without the permission of the publisher.

Library of Congress Cataloging in Publication Data

Al-Ghani, K. I.

Making the move : a guide for schools and parents on the transfer of pupils with autism spectrum disorders (ASDs) from primary to secondary school / K.I. Al-Ghani and Lynda Kenward ; illustrated by Haitham Al-Ghani.

p. cm.

ISBN 978-1-84310-934-1 (pb : alk. paper)

1. Autistic children--Education. 2. Students, Transfer of. I. Kenward, Lynda. II. Title.

LC4717.A4 2009

371.94--dc22

2008042698

British Library Cataloguing in Publication Data

A CIP catalogue record for this book is available from the British Library

ISBN 978 1 84310 934 1

Printed and bound in Great Britain by
Printwise (Haverhill) Ltd, Suffolk

Hench
Autism
LC
4717
.A4
2009

JUN 2 2 2009

VDMƏM

About the authors

Kay Al-Ghani is a special educational needs teacher who has worked for more than 30 years in the field of education. She is currently a specialist teacher for inclusion support and is involved with training professionals, students and parents in aspects of ASD. As an author and mother of a son with ASD, she has spent the last twenty years researching the enigma that is autism.

Lynda Kenward has over thirty years' experience of working in special education. Now retired, her recent role as specialist teacher for inclusion support has motivated a particular interest in developing visual resources for children with ASD.

About the illustrator

Haitham Al-Ghani is 23 years of age. He earned a triple distinction in Multimedia Studies and was the 2007 winner of the Vincent Lines Award for creative excellence at Hastings College of Arts and Technology.

Haitham's struggle with Semantic/Pragmatic Disorder has given him a unique insight into the world of people with ASD. He is an author and illustrator and lives in Hastings, England.

Contents

Introduction

Transfer from primary to secondary school is a time of great anxiety for most children. Imagine how much more acute that anxiety could become if you suffer from an Autism Spectrum Disorder (ASD).

Fear of the unknown, the need for monumental changes and the inability to imagine a favourable outcome, can all combine to make this unavoidable step in school life a time of great fear and dread.

PRIMARY SCHOOL

ENTRANCE

SECONDARY SCHOOL

ENTRANCE

The need for scrupulous transfer arrangements is linked to the inability of the child with ASD to predict the outcome of any new situation. No matter how much discussion has taken place, it is only when the situation has been experienced first hand that they will have a real understanding of it and be able to build up what is termed a 'real-life memory bank' (RLMB).

The aim of this guidance is to ensure that any opportunities or preparation lead to a favourable outcome, in order to build a positive RLMB. The most effective strategies will encourage and inspire greater confidence for parents, pupils and schools.

All children with ASD present differently. Strategies and guidelines should be used at the discretion of the Special Educational Needs Coordinator (SENCO) and agreed by all adults involved with the child.

1 Planning the Move

It is important when planning the move from primary to secondary school, to ensure that all available options have been thoroughly researched. Choosing the right school, one that will meet your child's needs, is essential and so it is never too early to start visiting local secondary

schools to see what they have to offer. It would be a good idea to plan out a list of questions to ask each school; these could be formulated with the help of the school SENCO or class teacher. It could be that siblings may go to a particular school and so choice is limited. However, careful consideration in these early stages will empower the parents/carers to make the right choice.

It is not necessary to involve the child at this stage. It is probably better to make the choice of school and then let the child know when it is certain they will be attending.

2 Term by Term Planning

YEAR 5 – TERMS 5 AND 6

- Parents/carers should visit all appropriate secondary schools in order for them to make informed choices regarding placement.

- The parental/carer choices should then be discussed at the final Annual Review of Year 5 (for children with a statutory assessment) or at the final parent/teacher meeting for Year 5.

YEAR 6 – TERMS 1 AND 2

The final year at primary school is a time to take stock of the key skills that a child needs in order to make a smooth transition to a new school. It is important not to make assumptions where the child with ASD is concerned. Many skills may be underdeveloped or even non-existent, and so the class teacher should set targets for pupil knowledge, which should include the following.

The pupil should be able to:

- Tell the time on a watch and clock.

- Copy the date from a board.

- Know how to use a timetable.

- Keep a homework diary.

- Use a ruler.

- Pack the contents of a school bag by following a prompt list (see the example on page 67).

- Practise using a locker.

- Know how to use a library.

- Make independent choices for school dinners/snacks and to know dinner time procedures.

- Dress/undress without supervision for PE/swimming.

It is during this stage in the school year that a parent/carer conference will be held to discuss the choice of secondary school and to advise on form completion, if necessary.

Year 6 – Terms 3 and 4

By this time in the school year a decision regarding choice of school should have been reached and a placement organised. This is where the work of the SENCO is vital. Liaising with the new school and passing on information about the pupil profile is essential for a smooth transition. Parents/carers should have had the opportunity to discuss their child at length with the new school SENCO and ensure that a full profile is given to avoid difficulties later.

At this stage the SENCO should:

- Organise liaison between the confirmed secondary school and the primary school on transfer/visiting arrangements/strategies. Ensure that parents/carers are informed and involved.

- Ensure that teachers at the secondary school are aware of the use of language for children who have ASD, e.g. when giving verbal instructions:

  o   Keep it simple.

  o   Be specific.

  o   Be direct.

  o   Avoid using words like 'everybody' or 'everyone' – address the child by name before giving a verbal instruction.

  o   Avoid the use of rhetorical questions beginning 'can you?' or 'shall we?'.

- ○ Allow extra time for the child to process the information or request.

- ○ If you repeat yourself, use the same language.

- ○ Use a word audit to check that the child understands key words.

- ○ Whenever possible, use the visual to supplement the verbal.

It is at this time that the class teacher should begin to involve the pupil in preparation for the transfer. The school holiday prior to this term could be used to prepare the child with ASD for the forthcoming move to a new school. Parents/carers and siblings can begin to talk about the move and so when the child returns to school he or she will already be aware of what will happen at the end of the school year. Remember this is a stressful time for *all* children and so expect some tantrums and upsets. It is not uncommon for the child with ASD to declare that while everyone else is going to be moving to a new school, he or she will not be. Try not to get too emotional, simply state the facts and refuse to be caught up in angry outbursts. A Social Story™ could be very valuable at this stage. See pages 77–87 for an example.

Work can now begin in earnest to prepare the child for the changes. While some things about secondary school will be the same for the child, many things will be both new and confusing. A great deal of new vocabulary will need to be absorbed and understood by the child with ASD. To this end, the teacher should ensure that opportunities for assimilating these new things are made available during school time. Issues concerning school rules, behaviour, etc. can be addressed during circle times and planned into the PHSE (Personal, Health, Social and Emotional) curriculum since it will involve all pupils.

The class teacher should:

- Introduce secondary school subject areas and ensure the child can read and spell these and understand the content of each. (This could be achieved as a class project.)

- Begin preparation of the pupil for transfer. Refer to and start to fill in the 'My Move to Secondary School' workbook (pages 23–61).

YEAR 6 – TERMS 5 AND 6

This is the final countdown and the SENCO should make the following arrangements:

- Request a key worker from the secondary school to liaise with parents and address any concerns. (This could be achieved through e-mail.)

- Arrange visits for the child to view the secondary school, meet the staff and take photographs/ film, preferably with his/her Individual Needs Assistant (INA). Visits should allow for experience of school life throughout the day.

- SENCO to liaise with secondary school and parents and agree on support strategies, such as:

  - Visual support resources.

  - Break times.

  - Transition times.

  - Safe haven.

  - Home/school liaison and the importance of this, particularly for terms 1 and 2 of Year 7.

  - Buddy system. Distant support might be more appropriate for children who are uncomfortable with a close proximity buddy.

  - Homework. This should be treated as a school subject. A homework folder could be used and collected at the end of the school day. Ensure that any resources needed to complete the homework task are available.

- SENCO to advise parents on preparation during the summer break.

- Continue with completion of the 'My Move to Secondary School' workbook and introduce relevant visual resources from the selection provided.

3 Summer Break

- Ensure that the Social Story™, 'My Secondary School', photographs of the secondary school and the workbook 'My Move to Secondary School' are available for frequent referral.

- Frequently play any film you may have taken of the school.

- Buy and label school uniform/sports and swimming kits, school equipment, etc. (If at all possible buy duplicates of items chosen by the child, e.g. pencil case, lunchbox, etc. It is not unusual for items to go missing and some children can become quite distraught if the same item is then unavailable.)

- Allow the child to practise trying on the new school uniform, on several occasions. It may be necessary to teach him or her how to do up a tie – this could be made into a game with suitable rewards.

- Encourage the child to enrol in any summer projects run by the secondary school.

In the week before the new term:

- Encourage the child to get up at the same time as a school day.

- Prepare the school bag well in advance of the first day.

4 My Move to Secondary School

The workbook has been written for a child with ASD, but its use would be beneficial for any child who requires additional support for the transition from primary to secondary school.

This section will provide the child with key information about the secondary school. It should be completed by the child with the support of his or her teacher, Individual Needs Assistant (INA) and parents/carer.

The workbook should be supplemented with photographs and perhaps some film footage of the secondary school. If at all possible, the child should be responsible for these.

It is a workbook that can be used with any child, so the teacher may decide to make this a class or group activity and in this way the child will not be singled out.

It is important not to rush into filling out this workbook. It could be presented as individual pages rather than a whole workbook.

It is hoped that at the end of the exercise the child will take ownership and be able to use it to dispel any fears about the move by making the secondary school environment as familiar as possible. It should have a self-calming effect similar to a Social Story™.

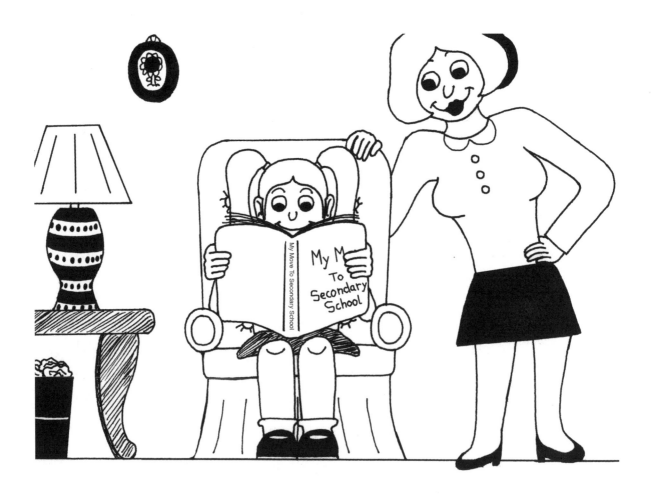

My Move to Secondary School

Name:..

Copyright © K.I. Al-Ghani and Lynda Kenward 2009

✓

Here is my secondary school

Stick a photograph of your
secondary school here

It is called ....

Copyright © K.I. Al-Ghani and Lynda Kenward 2009

All about me

Stick a photograph
of yourself here

My name is ....

My birthday is on ....

I am good at...

....

....

....

My favourite sports are..

....

....

....

Widgit Symbols © Widgit Software 2008 PCS symbols © Mayer Johnson LLC
Contact Widgit Software www.widgit.com

My   favourite   foods   are ....

....

....

....

My   favourite   TV   programmes   are.....................

....

....

....

Widgit Symbols © Widgit Software 2008 PCS symbols © Mayer Johnson LLC
Contact Widgit Software www.widgit.com

My favourite toys are...

....

....

....

My favourite movies are...

....

....

....

Widgit Symbols © Widgit Software 2008 PCS symbols © Mayer Johnson LLC
Contact Widgit Software www.widgit.com

My favourite books are..

....

....

....

My favourite people are...

....

....

....

Widgit Symbols © Widgit Software 2008 PCS symbols © Mayer Johnson LLC
Contact Widgit Software www.widgit.com

Will I know anyone at my secondary school?

....

....

....

Make a list of people you know:

Brother ....

Sister...

Widgit Symbols © Widgit Software 2008 PCS symbols © Mayer Johnson LLC
Contact Widgit Software www.widgit.com

Children from my primary school ....

....

....

....

....

Others ....

....

....

....

Widgit Symbols © Widgit Software 2008 PCS symbols © Mayer Johnson LLC
Contact Widgit Software www.widgit.com

✓

What after school activities are available?

....

....

....

....

....

....

....

....

....

Widgit Symbols © Widgit Software 2008 PCS symbols © Mayer Johnson LLC
Contact Widgit Software www.widgit.com

I would enjoy doing these activities:

....

....

....

....

....

....

....

....

....

What is the name of your secondary school?

....

....

....

What is the name of the headteacher?

....

....

....

Widgit Symbols © Widgit Software 2008 PCS symbols © Mayer Johnson LLC
Contact Widgit Software www.widgit.com

What are the names of your class and subject teachers?
Make a list:

....

....

....

....

How many children are there at secondary school?

....

....

....

You will meet lots of new people at secondary school.

Widgit Symbols © Widgit Software 2008 PCS symbols © Mayer Johnson LLC
Contact Widgit Software www.widgit.com

List three things you could do to make a friend:

1 ....

2 ....

3 ....

Widgit Symbols © Widgit Software 2008 PCS symbols © Mayer Johnson LLC
Contact Widgit Software www.widgit.com

What subjects will you be doing at secondary school?

....

....

....

....

....

....

....

....

....

Widgit Symbols © Widgit Software 2008 PCS symbols © Mayer Johnson LLC
Contact Widgit Software www.widgit.com

? 🕐   🧑📋   👨‍👩‍👧🏠

How long are the lessons at secondary school?

....

....

....

? 😊✓   🧑📋   ⇒

How will you know when the lesson is finished?

....

....

....

Widgit Symbols © Widgit Software 2008 PCS symbols © Mayer Johnson LLC
Contact Widgit Software www.widgit.com

Look at the plan of your secondary school.

Stick it on this page:

Widgit Symbols © Widgit Software 2008 PCS symbols © Mayer Johnson LLC
Contact Widgit Software www.widgit.com

 Can you find:

the science lab?

the art room?

the music room?

Widgit Symbols © Widgit Software 2008 PCS symbols © Mayer Johnson LLC
Contact Widgit Software www.widgit.com

assembly hall?

the gym?

the dining room?

your   classroom?

Widgit Symbols © Widgit Software 2008 PCS symbols © Mayer Johnson LLC
Contact Widgit Software www.widgit.com

Take a photograph of your school uniform, stick it here:

Does the school have a house or team system?

....

....

....

....

....

....

....

....

Widgit Symbols © Widgit Software 2008 PCS symbols © Mayer Johnson LLC
Contact Widgit Software www.widgit.com

Which   team   or   house   will   you   be   in?

....

....

?

What   will   you   do   at   morning   break time?

....

....

....

....

Widgit Symbols © Widgit Software 2008 PCS symbols © Mayer Johnson LLC
Contact Widgit Software www.widgit.com

Where will you go?

....

....

....

....

Widgit Symbols © Widgit Software 2008 PCS symbols © Mayer Johnson LLC
Contact Widgit Software www.widgit.com

Will you have a school dinner or take a packed lunch?

....

....

....

Widgit Symbols © Widgit Software 2008 PCS symbols © Mayer Johnson LLC
Contact Widgit Software www.widgit.com

What are the arrangements for lunchtimes?

....

....

....

....

....

....

....

....

Widgit Symbols © Widgit Software 2008 PCS symbols © Mayer Johnson LLC
Contact Widgit Software www.widgit.com

You could stick a photograph here of the

place you will eat lunch

Sometimes things go wrong.

What will you do if you lose or forget your

dinner money?

....

....

....

....

....

Widgit Symbols © Widgit Software 2008 PCS symbols © Mayer Johnson LLC
Contact Widgit Software www.widgit.com

Cannot find the room for the next lesson?

....

....

....

....

Forget or lose your pencil case?

....

....

....

Widgit Symbols © Widgit Software 2008 PCS symbols © Mayer Johnson LLC
Contact Widgit Software www.widgit.com

Do not understand your homework? ....

....

....

....

Can you think of other things that might go wrong?

X

....

....

....

Widgit Symbols © Widgit Software 2008 PCS symbols © Mayer Johnson LLC
Contact Widgit Software www.widgit.com

Make a list and say what you would do:

....

....

....

....

....

....

....

....

Widgit Symbols © Widgit Software 2008 PCS symbols © Mayer Johnson LLC
Contact Widgit Software www.widgit.com

Who could you go to if you need help? ....

....

....

....

....

Widgit Symbols © Widgit Software 2008 PCS symbols © Mayer Johnson LLC
Contact Widgit Software www.widgit.com

What are the arrangements for the first day of

secondary school?

....

....

....

?

What do you think you will like about your

secondary school?

List three things:

....

....

....

....

....

....

Widgit Symbols © Widgit Software 2008 PCS symbols © Mayer Johnson LLC
Contact Widgit Software www.widgit.com

Is there anything you are worried about?

....

....

....

....

....

....

 Talk to an adult. They will be able to help you.

Widgit Symbols © Widgit Software 2008 PCS symbols © Mayer Johnson LLC
Contact Widgit Software www.widgit.com

Why do schools have rules?

....

....

....

....

....

....

....

....

....

Widgit Symbols © Widgit Software 2008 PCS symbols © Mayer Johnson LLC
Contact Widgit Software www.widgit.com

Stick a copy of your school rules here:

Widgit Symbols © Widgit Software 2008 PCS symbols © Mayer Johnson LLC
Contact Widgit Software www.widgit.com

Think about what might happen if you forget a rule.

You could fill in the chart on the next page.

Widgit Symbols © Widgit Software 2008 PCS symbols © Mayer Johnson LLC
Contact Widgit Software www.widgit.com

School Rules

Rule	What might happen if I forget it

Copyright © K.I. Al-Ghani and Lynda Kenward 2009

5 Resources

- Mood diary

- Contents of school bag/prompt list

- Homework timetable

- Homework completed

- Ready for bed card

- Calendar

Mood diary

A mood diary can be used during the first few days or weeks to judge how the child feels on any given day. It is a useful tool to track any times during the school week that the child may find stressful or that are causing anxiety. As it only requires a tick in the appropriate box, it will not be necessary to talk about issues causing concern until the child is more composed. Sometimes the child may not be able to give voice to any concerns and so by doing a little detective work it may be possible to find out what is causing distress or anxiety on any given day.

Mood diary

Day/Date		Happy	Sad	Worried	Angry	Bored	Teacher/ TA comments
Monday	am						
	pm						
Tuesday	am						
	pm						
Wednesday	am						
	pm						
Thursday	am						
	pm						
Friday	am						
	pm						

Copyright © K.I. Al-Ghani and Lynda Kenward 2009
Illustrator copyright © Haitham Al-Ghani 2009

CONTENTS OF THE SCHOOL BAG

We have lost count of the number of times we have been called into school meetings concerning a child with ASD and the problem of the school bag. For those of us who live and/or work with these children we know they are very protective of their possessions. Anxiety over what is in the bag can lead to constant checking of the contents that can drive even the most patient teacher to the point of despair!

The prompt list can be duplicated and laminated, one copy for home and one for school. Encourage the child to check off the items in the bag the evening before school. At school he or she can then check off what is needed for any particular lesson, and then the bag can be put safely away until the items are to be put back. Quite often, as the child becomes used to the school routine, he or she no longer feels the need to check every item rigorously.

It may be a good idea to buy several of the same item, in case something goes missing. This way it can be replaced with minimal fuss.

Contents of school bag – prompt list

Have I got...	✓					
Pencil case						
Ruler						
Eraser						
Pens						
Pencils						
Crayons						
Sharpener						
Maths equipment						
Mood diary						
Homework folder						
Dinner money/ packed lunch						
Home/school diary						
P.E. kit		Monday	Tuesday	Wednesday	Thursday	Friday
Swimming kit		Monday	Tuesday	Wednesday	Thursday	Friday
Timetable						
Bus fare						
Snack/money						
Subject books						
Tissues						
Dictionary						
Other/e.g. medicine/project						

Copyright © K.I. Al-Ghani and Lynda Kenward 2009

HOMEWORK

Clear guidelines regarding homework are essential when making the move from primary to secondary school. The child may not have had to do much homework at primary school and so it is often a cause of great upset for both parents/carers and children.

For children with ASD, coming home after a hard day at school is a welcome relief. They will have their own routine to help them to unwind and it is often a time when tempers flare up. By making homework like a school subject, it is possible to set up a routine that the child will adhere to and that can earn him or her valuable rewards and praise. As such, it should be included on the child's visual timetable at school so that he or she knows that there will be work to do on arriving home.

Once the routine is established, it is possible to make homework times both enjoyable and productive. A clear homework timetable is important to this end. Class and subject teachers should be aware of the need to stick to the timetable and to ensure that the child knows exactly what he or she needs to do, when to do it and when to hand it in.

Having the necessary resources to complete a task is also essential. We know many parents who resort to doing the homework themselves! This is obviously not the ideal and by just making sure everything is in place and clear guidelines are adhered to, it is possible to make homework a positive experience.

The class teacher can be encouraged to differentiate the homework tasks for children with ASD, since problems relating to a lack of organisational skills, difficulty with penmanship and distractibility, can all combine to make homework tasks a lengthy and stressful experience.

Homework timetable

Subject	Maths	English	Science	French	German	Spanish	Geog	History	DT	RE	Art	Music	PSHE	ICT	Other
Monday															
Tuesday															
Wednesday															
Thursday															
Friday															

To be handed in on:

Homework timetable

Subject	Maths	English	Science	French	German	Spanish	Geog	History	DT	RE	Art	Music	PSHE	ICT	Other
Monday															
Tuesday															
Wednesday															
Thursday															
Friday															

Copyright © K.I. Al-Ghani and Lynda Kenward 2009

The use of a visual timetable and perhaps a sand timer can help to give the child structure and the confidence to know that homework time will eventually come to an end!

It is possible to extend the child's concentration time just by sitting with the child and doing something unobtrusive like reading. In this way you are on hand to help if necessary, but are otherwise engaged, so he or she can get on with the task.

Homework completed

Date	Parent/Carer signature	Teacher signature/comment

Copyright © K.I. Al-Ghani and Lynda Kenward 2009

GETTING READY FOR BED

This is an especially stressful time in most households. A little trick that has proved most successful is the 'Getting Ready for Bed Card'. Here's where you hand over the nagging to a favourite cartoon or TV character. For example, if your child is especially fond of Dr Who, then Dr Who will take over the bedtime nagging.

On a small card put a picture of Dr Who. Underneath it write:

Dr Who says it is time for bed.

Is your uniform ready?

Have you got any kit you may need ready?

Is your homework in your school bag?

Is all your equipment in your school bag?

Dr Who says brilliant!

If you go to bed immediately, then you can watch one episode of Dr Who while eating breakfast. [*This also acts as in incentive to get up in the morning.*]

Dr Who says: Goodnight!

Used effectively one does not have to say anything – just present the card.

The card is then used in the morning to redeem the reward.

Getting ready
for bed card

....................................says it is time for bed.

Stick a picture of favourite

character here

....................................asks:

Is your uniform ready?

Copyright © K.I. Al-Ghani and Lynda Kenward 2009

Have you got any kit you may need ready?

Is your homework in your school bag?

Is all your equipment in your school bag?

....says brilliant!

If you go to bed immediately, then you can watch one episode of .... while eating breakfast.

....says: Goodnight!

Copyright © K.I. Al-Ghani and Lynda Kenward 2009

Calendar

Month: _____

Year: _____

Sunday	Monday	Tuesday	Wednesday	Thursday	Friday	Saturday

Copyright © K.I. Al-Ghani and Lynda Kenward 2009

6 Social Stories™

Social Stories™ have proved to be most effective in giving children (Carol Gray – Social Stories™) with ASD a means to promote greater understanding, to self-calm and increase self-awareness, in any given situation. They should be specific to the child and follow a strict format.

A sample Social Story™ has been included, but parents and schools should work together to ensure that the story meets the needs of the child.

SAMPLE SOCIAL STORY ™

Use one page for each sentence. Add photographs, illustrations, additional symbols, etc. to make the story more personal and meaningful.

My Secondary School

Photograph of the school

Copyright © K.I. Al-Ghani and Lynda Kenward 2009

✓

At the end of Year 6, all children leave primary school and move to secondary school.

Copyright © K.I. Al-Ghani and Lynda Kenward 2009

Some things will be the same as at primary school and some things will be different.

Copyright © K.I. Al-Ghani and Lynda Kenward 2009

✓

My teacher and my family are helping me to know all about my secondary school.

Copyright © K.I. Al-Ghani and Lynda Kenward 2009

I will have photographs/a film to look at.

Copyright © K.I. Al-Ghani and Lynda Kenward 2009

I will have 'My move to Secondary School' booklet to read.

Copyright © K.I. Al-Ghani and Lynda Kenward 2009

I will try to remember to read 'My Move to Secondary School' booklet and look at the photographs/film to remind me about my secondary school.

Copyright © K.I. Al-Ghani and Lynda Kenward 2009

Then I will be ready for Year 7 at my secondary school.

Copyright © K.I. Al-Ghani and Lynda Kenward 2009

Moving to a secondary school is okay.

Widgit Symbols © Widgit Software 2008 PCS symbols © Mayer Johnson LLC
Contact Widgit Software www.widgit.com

7 A Word about Siblings

While we have concentrated primarily on the needs of the child with ASD, mention should be made of siblings. Older siblings at school may be anxious about the effect of the move on their own school life. While they should be encouraged to give help and advice, they should in no way be made responsible for the success of the move or for any problems that occur at school. They should be allowed to continue as normal, have lunch and break times with their own friends and not be called on for help or advice by the school. Parents and school staff should be aware that siblings may need to express their thoughts, feelings and concerns, before, during and after transition.

Not everything should revolve around the world of the child with ASD. Siblings need to know that they are special, too!

THE LAST WORD:

The key to a successful transition between primary and secondary school for children with ASDs is the provision of the four R's:

ROUTINE

RITUAL

REPETITION

RESOURCES

- Parents/carers need to establish the daily routines.

- Teachers need to add daily rituals (e.g. a short burst of classical music to signal the end of a lesson).

- The children need plenty of opportunities for repetition.

- Finally use visual resources wherever possible.

It is hoped that the provision of these four crucial elements will lead to a happy and successful move and greater independence for the child with ASD.

Index

The Red Beast
Controlling Anger in Children with Asperger's Syndrome
K.I. Al-Ghani
Illustrated by Haitham Al-Ghani
Hardback, ISBN 978 1 84310 943 3, 48 pages

Deep inside everyone, a red beast lies sleeping.

When it is asleep, the red beast is quite small, but when it wakes up, it begins to grow and grow.

This is the story of how one boy, Rufus, conquered his anger and sent the red beast back to sleep.

Developed in conjunction with the National Autistic Society (NAS), this book offers a range of anger management strategies and useful guidance for parents on how to help their child 'tame the red beast'.

K.I. Al-Ghani is a Special Educational Needs teacher and consultant who has worked for more than 30 years in the field of Education. As a teacher and the mother of a child with an Autistic Spectrum Disorder, she has spent many years developing strategies to help children cope with the stress of life both in the classroom and at home.

Haitham Al-Ghani is 22 years of age and is on the autism spectrum. He has recently completed full-time education after earning a triple distinction in Multimedia Studies and winning the Vincent Lines Award for creative excellence, at Hastings College of Arts and Technology.

How to Make School Make Sense
A Parents' Guide to Helping the Child with
Asperger Syndrome
Clare Lawrence
Foreword by Tony Attwood
Paperback, ISBN 978 1 84310 664 7, 128 pages

"My face was smiling all the time I was reading it, thinking, 'Yes, that's great advice.'
An excellent book."

—Professor Tony Attwood

"*How to Make School Make Sense* adopts a refreshingly honest and realistic approach. Outlining practical and achievable changes that parents can instigate themselves, it helps parents gain confidence that they can make their child's life at school a less bewildering and altogether happier experience."

—Dr. Rebecca Chilvers, University College London

"We seldom realise how alien and unwelcoming school can be to kids on the spectrum. *How to Make School Make Sense* had me involved and thinking throughout. It offers many concrete suggestions and guides the mind to create one's own solutions; a most useful resource."

—Jan Campito, author of Supportive Parenting: Becoming an Advocate for Your Child with Special Needs

Every child's education relies on a partnership between parents, professionals and, of course, the child. This book gives parents of children with Asperger syndrome (AS) practical advice on how to make the most of this important partnership and how to work with schools to ensure their child's needs are being met.

The book explores how parents can prepare their child for school life and how they can work with teachers to improve the classroom environment, as well as the school environment as a whole, for their child and consequently for the benefit of all pupils. Strategies include peer education, the use of visual cues and rules, and effective communication between parents, teachers and support staff.

This clear, accessible book will be an invaluable guide for parents of children with AS and will also be of interest to the teachers and educational professionals who work with them.

Clare Lawrence is a teacher and mother of two children, one of whom has Asperger syndrome. Clare is a graduate of Oxford, York, Northumbria, Sheffield Hallam and Birmingham universities, and has a University Certificate in autism spectrum disorders and a post-graduate certificate in Asperger syndrome. For the last four years she has been working closely with schools and exploring practical solutions on how to make school make sense for children with Asperger Syndrome.

**Reaching and Teaching the Child
with Autism Spectrum Disorder
Using Learning Preferences and Strengths**
Heather MacKenzie
Paperback, ISBN 978 1 84310 623 4, 272 pages

'This is an entertaining, informative and very practical book that will assist readers to "walk the talk" through a positive paradigm for enabling children with autism. It is based on careful and systematic thinking by the author and incorporates methodology based on research and best practice experience.'

– Carmen Hengeveld, M.Sc., Registered Speech-Language Pathologist

'Dr Heather MacKenzie has used a unique blend of theories of personality type, multiple intelligences and mediated learning to create an elegant and practical method. I have seen how well the application of the Learning Preferences and Strengths model works for children with autism. It is my firm belief that this method has broad applicability for any learner.'

– Teeya Scholten, PhD, Registered Psychologist, Alberta, Canada

'This is a practical, inspiring and stimulating book.'

– Allison Waks, M.A., Registered Psychologist

Reaching and Teaching Children with Autism provides a positive approach to understanding and educating children on the autism spectrum. The book gives greater insight into the perspective and behavior of a child with autism and explores how the child's learning preferences, strengths and interests can be used to facilitate learning and enhance motivation.

Based on well-researched theory and extensive clinical experience, the author provides a comprehensive model for developing lifelong independent learning skills in children with autism between the ages of 3 and 12 years old. The book describes the underlying principles, learning preferences and strengths typical of children with autism and offers a detailed but flexible program structure based on these concepts. Easy-to-follow activities and approaches are described in each chapter, along with clear examples and illustrations.

This accessible and practical book is an essential resource for parents, teachers, support workers, therapists and others concerned with learning and development in children with autism.

Heather MacKenzie, PhD, a speech-language pathologist and educator by profession, has spent the past fifteen years of her 30-year career understanding the enigma of autism spectrum disorders (ASDs). She has developed a Learning Preferences and Strengths model designed to determine each child's learning preferences and strengths and then 'harness' them to improve the child's learning and development. Heather established a preschool program for children with ASD based on this model.

Hints and Tips for Helping Children with Autism Spectrum Disorders
Useful Strategies for Home, School, and the Community
Dion E. Betts and Nancy J. Patrick
Paperback, ISBN 978 1 84310 896 2, 192 pages

If you have a child on the autism spectrum who struggles with the challenges of daily life, then this book is for you! *Hints and Tips…* is peppered with vignettes and stories of real-life situations and successes, and offers clever ideas for tackling everyday difficulties, such as bathing, bedtime, school trips, and selecting the right child minder.

Dion E. Betts and Nancy J. Patrick provide creative, practical strategies to help parents and caregivers to support their child, and to enable their child to develop the social skills needed to manage and enjoy daily life to the fullest. The book is split into five parts: home life, hygiene, community, medical, and schools and organizations. Common problem areas are also tackled in a toolkit section, which includes checklists, 'to do' lists, visual schedules, and mnemonics to aid memory and retrieval.

Hints and Tips for Helping Children with Autism Spectrum Disorders is an essential aid for parents and carers to make small and simple changes that result in big improvements in the quality of life for children, their families, and carers.

Dion E. Betts, Ed.D., is a special education administrator, adjunct professor, writer, and presenter. He and his wife have five children, one of whom has Asperger Syndrome. They live in Lancaster, Pennsylvania. **Nancy J. Patrick**, Ph.D., is Assistant Professor of Special Education at Messiah College, Grantham, Pennsylvania. She is both a certified school psychologist and licensed psychologist, as well as an author, teacher, writer, and presenter. She lives near Harrisburg, Pennsylvania, with her husband and their three children, one of whom has a disability.

Create a Reward Plan for your Child with Asperger Syndrome
John Smith, Jane Donlan and Bob Smith
Paperback, ISBN 978 1 84310 622 7, 112 pages

Reward plans encourage positive behaviour using the incentive of earning rewards. This book provides a thorough nuts-and-bolts guide to creating a reward plan for your child with Asperger Syndrome (AS) to help him or her develop positive behaviours, such as social and communication skills.

John Smith, Jane Donlan and their son Bob, who was diagnosed with AS at age eight, explain the importance of keeping a reward plan positive, specific and challenging enough to be stimulating. Helping your child to learn about positive behaviour while gaining a sense of achievement, a reward plan increases self-esteem, confidence and independence.

Create a Reward Plan for your Child with Asperger Syndrome is full of advice and practical suggestions for how to tailor a reward plan to meet your child's specific needs.

John Smith is a mental health social worker and father of Bob. **Jane Donlan** is Bob's mum and is responsible for Bob's home education. **Bob Smith** is twelve years old and was diagnosed with Asperger Syndrome at age eight. He, his parents and his dogs live in the north of England.